The Inspiration Collection:

45 DEVOTIONS TO MOTIVATE & REJUVENATE YOU

Dr. Bryan K. Williams
KEYNOTE SPEAKER & AUTHOR

TABLE OF CONTENTS

The Inspiration Collection

The Affirmation Collection

MESSAGE FROM THE AUTHOR

An inspired person can achieve unimaginable feats. I am a big believer in tapping into the inner power that excites us and propels us forward. The vast majority of this book was written between March 2020 and July 2021. You might recognize that time frame as the period of COVID-19. As you'll recall, many of us felt down and even depressed. Anxiety and stress were at an all-time high.

Around March of 2020, I did my best to counteract the tsunami of negative news by writing inspirational articles and affirmations. Thus, this book is a compilation of what poured out of me in the hopes that, at least, one word would inspire, at least, one person.

You will notice that the chapters are concise and digestible. More importantly, there is a Key Takeaway at the end of each chapter. Don't skim past it. Don't gloss over it. That Key Takeaway is the golden nugget that I hope will connect with you. Of course, you may have other takeaways that resonate with you even more.

There is a brief series of questions, per chapter, to help guide you in articulating your action step(s). After all, for this book to be of any value, there must be a sustainable and noticeable shift in your life. Something should be better about you in some way.

So, my ultimate prayer for this book is for the Inspiration Collection to move you...so that you may move others.

To your success!

Bryan K. Williams, DM

DEDICATION

This book is dedicated to my loving parents, David & Thelma. Their never-ending belief in me laid the foundation for every dream I've had the audacity to strive for.

WHAT IS YOUR
name?

What is your name? How do you say it? How do you spell it?

Is your voice strong when you say it? Or does it waver? No matter what you may think, your name means something. It's a declaration that you are here and are meant to be acknowledged. Otherwise, no name is needed.

But YOU are needed.

Even if today seems darker than yesterday, YOU are needed. Even if you don't know what your next step should be, YOU are needed. You are necessary.

Someway - Somehow - This world is blessed by your existence.

The road ahead may seem like a mountain at times. But, here's the key: The mountain can either stop you or move you. The choice is yours.

Whenever you help someone, you move mountains. Whenever you encourage someone, you move mountains. Whenever you bring your smile into a room, you move mountains.

Mountains don't move you. You move mountains!

No matter what today brings...keep moving, keep striving, and Keep Saying Your Name.

KEY TAKEAWAY:

You are

NECESSARY.

How can the main theme of today's message apply to my life?

What is one thing I will start, stop or continue doing as a result of today's message?

Who can I share today's message with so they might benefit also?

Additional Notes:

EVEN
now.

It's easy to rejoice when things are going well. Anyone can have hope when there are tangible reasons to be hopeful. Prosperity has a way of bringing out the supreme optimism in us.

However, I've learned that the true test of my faith is what I focus on when things don't go so well.

Do I instantly forget all of the good that I enjoyed or do I remind myself of how fortunate I have been?

Do I lament about what I've lost or do I appreciate what I have?

Do I get angry at the world or do I find reasons to bring light into it?

Whenever an un-favorable season comes, I've created a habit out of using two words to press forward: Even Now.

Even now, I am still strong.

Even now, I have value.

Even now, I refuse to give up.

Even now, I will give thanks for what I have.

Even now, I am hopeful for brighter days.

Even now, I won't allow despair to take root.

Even now, I am loved.

Even now, I will love.

When circumstances are dark and disappointments come flooding my way, I will stand firm and say, "Even now, I am a child of God, and there will ALWAYS be a way."

KEY TAKEAWAY:
Even now,
I AM LOVED.

How can the main theme of today's message apply to my life?

What is one thing I will start, stop or continue doing as a result of today's message?

Who can I share today's message with so they might benefit also?

Additional Notes:

SPECIAL AND DIFFERENT
for a reason.

Many years ago, when I was in the 3rd grade, I was walking home from school.

As I was passing by one particular house (like I did everyday), an elderly lady came out to the fence, looked at me VERY intently and said, "I can tell that you are not like the other children. You are very polite, but I also see them teasing you because of your stutter. You are special and different for a reason!"

I thank God for that lady.

I've never forgotten that day, and little did I know that I'd become a professional speaker years later. You may not know the reasons for why you went through what you did, but you MUST know that you are special and different for a reason!

Don't rob the world of the brilliance that is YOU. Be unapologetically you. Don't try to sound like anyone...write like anyone...speak like anyone...dress like anyone...or think like anyone.

There are words this world will never hear unless YOU say them. There are things this world will never see unless YOU create them.

That is how unique you are. BORN to be that way. Other people might not understand you. That's ok. Don't let their lack of understanding make you think that you're unworthy.

Yes, you ARE worthy!

Yes, you ARE blessed!

Yes, you ARE strong!

Yes, you ARE a child of God!

Everyday. All day. Be You.

KEY TAKEAWAY:

Everyday.

ALL DAY.

Be You.

How can the main theme of today's message apply to my life?

What is one thing I will start, stop or continue doing as a result of today's message?

Who can I share today's message with so they might benefit also?

Additional Notes:

CALL IT BY ITS
name.

"Call it by its name."

So what exactly is "it"? (I thought you'd never ask).

IT is anything that has consistently gotten in your way to thriving.

IT is something that you try to keep hidden...or lie about.

IT is something that you sneak away to do.

IT has nothing to do with anyone else (It's your private burden).

IT is something that you know you shouldn't be doing.

IT hovers over your head like a dark cloud.

IT leaves you feeling low, weak, and stuck in a cycle of shame.

The first step in dealing with your IT is to call it out.

This is not the time for "Well, it's not that bad."

Yes, it is.

If the secrecy is stifling you, call it out. If it negatively affects you spiritually, financially or physically (health), call it out.

IT will make you believe that it's impossible to be liberated. Lies. You are divinely orchestrated to do something extraordinary in this world. And IT makes you feel less than ordinary. Less than the masterpiece that you were created to be.

So call it by its name. IT has held you back far too long.

KEY TAKEAWAY:

Acknowledge it.
REJECT IT. THEN FIND
SOMETHING
Better.

How can the main theme of today's message apply to my life?

What is one thing I will start, stop or continue doing as a result of today's message?

Who can I share today's message with so they might benefit also?

Additional Notes:

WHEN YOU SAY NO,
mean it.

I don't know who this is for, but my hope is that it reaches whomever it is supposed to reach.

No. That is the only word I need you to focus on today.

I didn't start to truly live until I learned the power of no.

If it drains my energy...NO

If it lowers my self-esteem...NO

If it causes me to look at myself in shame...NO

If it causes me to lie and hide the truth...NO

If it destroys relationships with people I love...NO

If it compromises my integrity and what I stand for...NO

If it creates short-term gratification but leads to long-term depression...NO. NO. NO.

And when you say no, MEAN IT! Don't be wishy-washy. Being half-committed has never built anything that lasts.

Having the courage to consistently say no gave me the boldness to say YES in other areas. Areas that produce only good returns in my life...health, family, faith, and service.

KEY TAKEAWAY:

Today..whatever "it" is...

LOOK IT IN THE FACE...
WITH YOUR HEAD HELD
HIGH... *and say NO.*

How can the main theme of today's message apply to my life?

What is one thing I will start, stop or continue doing as a result of today's message?

Who can I share today's message with so they might benefit also?

Additional Notes:

PERSIST, ESPECIALLY WHEN *you don't feel like it.*

One of my favorite basketball players was Allen Iverson. Because of his smaller body frame (compared to other NBA players), a reporter once asked him if he lifted weights as part of his workout regimen. He replied, "Nah, they were too heavy." Classic!

Weights are, indeed, heavy. They can either slow you down or build you up. They can weaken you or strengthen you. Over my life, I've learned the value of letting go. Letting go of things, people and vices that consistently weighed me down.

I've discovered that there is power in declaring, "I don't want it. I don't need it."

When you are in a job, and it's obvious that you are unhappy and way past your expiration date: Don't want it. Don't need it.

Having a supposed friendship, when it's completely based on you giving and the other person taking: Don't want it. Don't need it.

Being enslaved to habits that threaten to rip away your self-worth: Don't want it. Don't need it.

Remove anything from your life that is threatening your piece of mind and productivity.

Weights used to weaken me, but now they strengthen me. They remind me to persist, especially when I don't feel like it.

KEY TAKEAWAY:

If it drains my energy ...NO.

How can the main theme of today's message apply to my life?

What is one thing I will start, stop or continue doing as a result of today's message?

Who can I share today's message with so they might benefit also?

Additional Notes:

PROTECT YOUR
zeal.

"THIS PLACE does not deserve the best I have to offer. I will come to work, only do what is expected of me, collect my paycheck, and go home." Do you know anyone like that? I do.

You cannot allow anyone (or any work environment) to rob you of your zeal to be exceptional.

Fight for your zeal!

As a professional, you must never grow tired of honoring your role, honoring other people and honoring yourself.

At some point, each person has to make a decision about how exceptional he/she wants to be, regardless of the work environment. It can be exhausting to constantly strive for excellence in a work environment that you can't stand to be in.

In that case, see if you can address your discontentment with the appropriate people... or find somewhere else to work. But don't just find "any place" to work. Search for a company that has values which mirror your own...an organization that you can believe in. It just makes it SO much easier to consistently put forth your best effort.

KEY TAKEAWAY:

Relentlessly protect

YOUR RIGHT TO SHINE.

How can the main theme of today's message apply to my life?

What is one thing I will start, stop or continue doing as a result of today's message?

Who can I share today's message with so they might benefit also?

Additional Notes:

THROUGH THE
fire.

"Through the fire. To the limit. To the wall."

(Those are lyrics from one of my favorite songs...from one of my all-time favorite singers: Chaka Khan.)

What are you willing to go through to get to what you envision? Or put another way...what are you willing to STOP so you can move on to what you need to START? There are some things that will never start in our lives until we make up our minds to stop certain things that hold us back.

Whether that "thing" is a behavior, habit or thought, if it holds you back, it's got to go!

Whatever your "thing" is, be clear about it. Don't be wishy-washy, and don't be apathetic. You've got to get it out of your life. Forcefully. Immediately.

Renounce it. Rebuke it. Remove it.

Books won't do it. Coaching won't do it. Classes won't do it. They may help, but the real deal is for YOU to decide TODAY to choose light over darkness. Vitality over weakness. Dignity over shame.

When you take that step, it will feel like fire. It will be uncomfortable. That's ok. Take another step. And then another. And another. Pretty soon, you will be through the fire and out on the other side.

IF you're serious enough, fire can not and will not stop you. So keep moving..." Right down to the wire. Even through the fire."

KEY TAKEAWAY:

Renounce it.

REBUKE IT.

Remove it.

How can the main theme of today's message apply to my life?

What is one thing I will start, stop or continue doing as a result of today's message?

Who can I share today's message with so they might benefit also?

Additional Notes:

YOUR BLESSED
place.

Certain things should bother you because they don't align with who you are. There are certain places you shouldn't go to, and certain people you shouldn't be with because they don't align with who you are.

Your internal compass should act as a filter that keeps you honest to who you claim to be and who you aspire to become. As a child, your parent or guardian may have been that filter for you, but now you have to be the one to protect your integrity.

When I'm not doing what I'm supposed to be doing, I've found that life speaks to me in whispers at first. Then, if I don't pay attention to the whispers, they grow louder. Of course, the procrastination in me tries to ignore the voice. But, it gets louder and louder until the voice can't be ignored any longer.

NEVER allow anyone, anything or anyplace move you away from what you stand for.

That is your BLESSED place!

Protect it. Appreciate it. Grow it.

KEY TAKEAWAY:

Protect it.

APPRECIATE IT.

Grow it.

How can the main theme of today's message apply to my life?

What is one thing I will start, stop or continue doing as a result of today's message?

Who can I share today's message with so they might benefit also?

Additional Notes:

DON'T
quit.

If you feel knocked down or discouraged, please know that you are not alone. We have all felt moments of despair during this season. Myself included. With that in mind, I have two words for you to focus on:

Don't Quit

You have come to far in life. Too many people sacrificed for you to make it to where you are. Generations of your ancestors fought through unimaginable atrocities just so that YOU can be here right now.

You can not give up. You MUST not give up. Program yourself to put a smile on your face and declare...this too shall pass!

Yes, last week may have been dark. Yes, yesterday a tear may have rolled down your face, but don't quit.

Even when that small voice whispers, "You can't make it"... or..."You're not worthy"...or "Your life will never get back to what it was"...I need you to square your shoulders, lift your chin and say "Not Today! I will not quit! My life has a purpose, and it is to grow into a mountain; not shrink to a grain of sand."

KEY TAKEAWAY:

As long as

there is life in you

...DON'T STOP MOVING

FORWARD.

How can the main theme of today's message apply to my life?

What is one thing I will start, stop or continue doing as a result of today's message?

Who can I share today's message with so they might benefit also?

Additional Notes:

SIGN YOUR
work.

When I was in grade school, students could not turn in their assignment unless they signed their work. Signing your work meant that you checked it and are proud of what you submitted. It meant something. By definition, a signature is a distinguishing feature, aspect or mark. No one has your signature! It is 100% completely unique to you. As you serve your customers everyday, it is imperative that you learn to "sign your work".

Ever since I was a little boy, I've always loved the globe. My Aunt Iona had one in her house, and I spent hours studying that globe. So when I worked in hotels, I always asked my guests where they were from. No matter where they were from, I could have a basic conversation with them about their home country or state. That was my signature!

Whenever I learned that a guest was celebrating a birthday or anniversary, I could pick a few flowers from the hotel's garden, and send to their room, along with a hand-written card. That was my signature!

What is your signature?

What is your personal stamp on how you serve? Is it how you smile? Is it how you anticipate needs? Is it how you tell jokes...or escort rather than point...or answer the phone with excellence? I can guarantee that you have a signature. Something that is unique to you. Now, you may not recognize it as a signature because it comes so natural to you; in your mind, it must not be special. It is so important to realize that your signature is prevalent and significant.

Own your signature! Write it everyday! Don't blend in...stand out! And as you sign your work, everyone else will have the awareness and the courage to sign their work also.

KEY TAKEAWAY:
What is your
SIGNATURE?

How can the main theme of today's message apply to my life?

What is one thing I will start, stop or continue doing as a result of today's message?

Who can I share today's message with so they might benefit also?

Additional Notes:

LAYOFFS.

Layoffs. Furloughs. Job eliminations.

Hurt. Disappointed. Let down.

You are ALLOWED to feel all of it. However, let those feelings be temporary and not define the rest of your life. The truth is that despite how you may feel, your value and identity were never intended to be tied to a company. You are who you are. You were created to make a meaningful difference...wherever you happen to be.

As long as you are alive, the full plan and purpose for your life has not been fulfilled. That, by itself, is a reason to get excited.

You are rare and unique! And wherever there is rarity, there is value. Therefore, YOU are valuable. That is true whether you've worked at a company for decades or a few months.

So don't spend too much time looking backwards at the door that closed. As much as you were emotionally tied to that door, there are other doors ahead of you that will VALUE YOU EVEN MORE.

I had to learn that lesson years ago...so I understand. I was at a company that I loved for many years (and still have great admiration for), but my new chapter did not FULLY begin until I "let go" of what was and reached forth for what could be.

So, get up, straighten yourself and move forward to the abundance of what lies ahead for you.

KEY TAKEAWAY:

Straighten yourself

AND MOVE FORWARD.

How can the main theme of today's message apply to my life?

What is one thing I will start, stop or continue doing as a result of today's message?

Who can I share today's message with so they might benefit also?

Additional Notes:

UNBREAKABLE.

UNBREAKABLE. What does that word even mean? Can not be broken? Invincible?

I recently found myself musing on that word until something hit me. How would you KNOW that something is unbreakable? A clear, marketing slogan? A money-back guarantee? A warranty?

I mean, how would you actually know that something CAN NOT be broken? The only way to really know if a building is unbreakable is if something hits it that should break it...but it doesn't.

It still stands strong.

The presence of immense adversity is what lets you know if something is unbreakable. Without the adversity, you would never really KNOW.

In your life, is it a relationship? Is it your walk with God? Is it your self-worth? I believe that everyone has, at least, one thing in their lives for which they are unbreakable. Some aspect where they refuse to bend...or give up...or lay down. There is strength in that area.

Find it. Claim it. Strengthen it.

KEY TAKEAWAY:

Find it.

CLAIM IT.

Strengthen it.

How can the main theme of today's message apply to my life?

What is one thing I will start, stop or continue doing as a result of today's message?

Who can I share today's message with so they might benefit also?

Additional Notes:

FIND YOUR
calling.

If you are currently open to work or considering a career change, do everything possible to find your ideal role. You've earned the right to do so!

I'm sure you know the types of roles that you "can" do; but the real question is...What SHOULD you be doing? Given your unique strengths and experiences, what are you specifically designed to do?

Ask yourself questions like:

- If I could create the perfect role for MYSELF, what would it look like? (Forget the existing job titles that exist.)
- What are my talents?
- What types of tasks GIVE me energy?
- What types of tasks DRAIN my energy?
- Do I enjoy working with people? If so, in what capacity?
- Do I love to lead others?
- Do I prefer to implement what someone else puts forth?
- Do I prefer to advise?
- Do I prefer to work on large or small teams?
- Do I prefer being autonomous, where I set my own direction and priorities?

NO ONE can answer those questions better than you. Describe YOUR role.

Then, either create a business out of it or pitch it to an organization that you would like to be a part of.

So don't settle for "a job". Instead, use this time to design YOUR job, and then you'll see your productivity, engagement and success go through the roof!

KEY TAKEAWAY:
Don't settle for
"A JOB".

How can the main theme of today's message apply to my life?

What is one thing I will start, stop or continue doing as a result of today's message?

Who can I share today's message with so they might benefit also?

Additional Notes:

USE YOUR
whole heart.

Some people believe that leaders have to be EITHER kind or tough. Not true at all. You can be both. In fact, I urge you to never feel like you have to explain your kindness or justify your high expectations.

The duality reflects your humanity. Love that about yourself.

Don't think that something is wrong if you have collegues who don't share your conviction, or encourage your zest for authentic leadership.

Be exceptional, anyway.

Know in your heart that leading with passion, purpose, and love is a beautiful thing. Challenge yourself to be an inspiration to those around you, even on days when you don't feel like it. It doesn't matter how passionate you are.

There will always be days when you would rather just do what you're supposed to do and go home. But you won't.

You were not born to do just the bare minimum. Only your best efforts will do.

KEY TAKEAWAY:

Put your whole heart

INTO HOW YOU LEAD

AND WHO YOU LEAD.

How can the main theme of today's message apply to my life?

What is one thing I will start, stop or continue doing as a result of today's message?

Who can I share today's message with so they might benefit also?

Additional Notes:

LESSONS I'VE
learned.

In all my years of living, here is what I've learned...

Nobody can stop me like me.

No one can get in my own way like I can.

There is not a person on Earth that can cast doubt on my life more effectively than myself.

Sure, it might be convenient to blame other people when I don't accomplish something.

Ultimately, though, I've learned that when my desire is strong enough, nothing can get in my way.

I have learned to be my own best advocate. My own best encourager. My own best motivator.

I've also learned the importance of saying "No"...to myself.

No to unhealthy urges, yearnings and temptations.

Saying no to myself requires discipline. It means loving myself enough to say: THAT has no place in my life.

Saying no means to zealously guard my eyes, ears, heart and mind from anything or anyone that drains me.

Saying no means knowing that immediate gratification often leads to long-term consequences. Whereas, delayed gratification often leads to long term peace-of-mind.

When I learned to say no, another door opened that I didn't even know existed.

That door led to me seeing myself as a blessed child of God, which simultaneously led me to view everyone else the same way.

KEY TAKEAWAY:

We are all

blessed...

WHETHER WE REALIZE IT OR NOT.

How can the main theme of today's message apply to my life?

What is one thing I will start, stop or continue doing as a result of today's message?

Who can I share today's message with so they might benefit also?

Additional Notes:

WHAT YOU
say.

What you SAY and what you DO are connected.

Strategic plans, vision boards and new year's resolutions are all great; however they all boil down to one simple truth:

If it's important, you make time for it. If it's not, you won't.

If it's important, nothing gets in your way. If it's not, every excuse seems logical.

If it's important, you put it on your schedule. If it's not, you will only make time when it's convenient.

If it's important, you will talk about it EVERYDAY. In fact, IF it's important, you won't even have to tell people that it's important; it will be OBVIOUS through your actions and what you ALWAYS talk about.

No one can "make" you believe that something is important. They can tell you, scold you and even punish you. But you still have to arrive at that sacred place and declare, "This is important; therefore, I will treat it as such." And when that happens, nothing (or no one) can stop you.

In Sept of 1992, I began the 11th grade and got a full-time job as a busboy in a fine-dining restaurant. I went to school during the day and worked the dinner shift at night. I usually finished work after midnight. Then got a ride home, and did homework until I fell asleep (after 2AM). Woke up at 7am. Caught the bus or caught a ride to school. Did school work before classes, during breaks and lunchtime. Did school work on weekends, and during my dinner break at work.

I was a C student for my entire academic career up to the 11th grade. My high school counselor told me that there was no way I could work full-time and pass my classes. I remember clearly saying to myself (and to her) that I would get a 100% on EVERY assignment, quiz, test and exam from that point until I graduated. I almost hit that goal. (I got a 98% on one test).

No one gave me that goal. I decided to do it. That experience taught me that goal-achievement has far more to do with DESIRE than capability. Basically, do you want it bad enough?

KEY TAKEAWAY:

Decide what is important to you,

AND DON'T STOP UNTIL YOU GET IT.

How can the main theme of today's message apply to my life?

What is one thing I will start, stop or continue doing as a result of today's message?

Who can I share today's message with so they might benefit also?

Additional Notes:

WHO WILL YOU MOTIVATE

today?

Whether you realize it or not, YOU are someone else's legacy. Someone else prayed for you, cried for you and interceded for you. It may have been a parent or it may have been a relative from many generations ago.

Despite what you may think about your current circumstance, you are the HOPE that your ancestors dreamed of. Their FAITH pushed you from where they were. And their LOVE still moves you when you feel like stopping.

So be unstoppable!

A motivated version of you is unstoppable. And you KNOW it. Look at what you've been through! Look at what you've had to deal with in your life. And, somehow, you are STILL here!!

Everything that you have been through has brought you to this point. Here is where you will leave a mark...evidence... a legacy that you were here.

Be someone who is known for multiplying the value of wherever you are. I have found that one of the best ways to add value is by motivating others. That is also one of the best ways to motivate yourself. Yes, by motivating others, you motivate yourself. By helping others, you help yourself. By loving others, you love yourself.

As you go through your day, the key question is not, "are you motivated?" The real question is…who will you motivate today?

KEY TAKEAWAY:

Are you

MOTIVATED?

How can the main theme of today's message apply to my life?

What is one thing I will start, stop or continue doing as a result of today's message?

Who can I share today's message with so they might benefit also?

Additional Notes:

WATCH YOUR *mouth.*

"Be careful what you say."
"Think before you speak."

We've all gotten those lessons at some point in our lives. The message is the same: What you SAY has power. Power to build and power to tear down. Power to transform and power to re-affirm.

Over the years, I have learned that the words I say to myself hit the hardest, and last the longest.

What you say to yourself...about yourself...matters. So watch your mouth.

Anything you repeatedly say to yourself, you will eventually believe... whether it's good or bad. Watch your mouth.

Who do you say you are? Who do you say you are not? Watch your mouth.

Are you proclaiming gratitude, health & prosperity? Or are you declaring resentment, sickness & hardship? Watch your mouth.

Do your words encourage you towards something better? Or do they discourage you towards something worse? Watch your mouth.

Train yourself to analyze every word that bubbles up inside of you. Your thoughts become your words, and then your words become your actions. So if you want to change your actions, you MUST change your words. And to change your words, you MUST change your thoughts.

Now here's the key. If you are SERIOUS about changing your thoughts, the most powerful way to do that is to:

Change. What. You. Say. To. Yourself.

KEY TAKEAWAY:

Think before

YOU SPEAK.

How can the main theme of today's message apply to my life?

What is one thing I will start, stop or continue doing as a result of today's message?

Who can I share today's message with so they might benefit also?

Additional Notes:

BE GRATEFUL
either way.

We're slammed! It's too busy! We are in the weeds! The lines are sooooo long! The phones won't stop ringing! Ugh!

Have you ever heard anyone say those things? Someone who complains when they are busy?

Now, pause and remember what it may have been like for you during the pandemic of 2020-2021. Maybe laid off or furloughed? Perhaps you were concerned if your industry would ever return to what it was?

The opposite of being busy is NOT having a job. So instead of complaining when we are busy, we must learn to be grateful when we are busy. Thankful when we are busy. Appreciative when we are busy.

Pause if you need to. Breathe if you must. But NEVER complain when prosperity comes your way.

It's interesting how some people pray for something to happen, then complain when it happens.

Lord, please help me get a house...then complain about cutting the grass.

Lord, help me get a car...then complain about having to wash it.

Lord, help me get a job...then complain about who you work with.

If you live long enough, you'll always notice that life is a series of hills and valleys.

KEY TAKEAWAY:

Prosperity is not constant;

NEITHER IS HARDSHIP.

How can the main theme of today's message apply to my life?

What is one thing I will start, stop or continue doing as a result of today's message?

Who can I share today's message with so they might benefit also?

Additional Notes:

TAKE THE
wheel.

What should we do when we know exactly what to do, but still don't do it?

What should we do when we know precisely what NOT to do, but do it anyway?

What should we do when we THINK we were in control, but come to find out that we are BEING controlled?

- *I've learned that if I have to hide it, I don't need it.*
- *If I have to lie about it, I don't need it.*
- *If it causes me to feel ashamed, I don't need it.*

Books, classes, coaching, you name it - they all have their role in helping us navigate out of the potholes that we REPEATEDLY and WILLINGLY drop in to.

But at some point, the only thing that will work is making a decision TODAY to not drop into that pothole TODAY. And each of us must make that decision because we know exactly how much hurt that pothole causes.

So, this is it. I know the roads that lead to the pothole, but now I am taking another road. That other road may seem longer and not as adventurous, but the view is so...much...better. The air is so much better. The sun's warmth is so much better. EVERYTHING is so much better.

I'm now riding on that better road. That higher road. That loving road. That encouraging road.

That rejuvenating road. That soul-satisfying road.

The only thing is now...I am not driving.

Jesus, has taken the wheel.

KEY TAKEAWAY:

Jesus,

HAS TAKEN THE WHEEL.

How can the main theme of today's message apply to my life?

What is one thing I will start, stop or continue doing as a result of today's message?

Who can I share today's message with so they might benefit also?

Additional Notes:

WHO DO YOU THINK
you are?

Who do you think you are? You've taken one step forward, but you've stumbled two steps backward.

You've thrived, and you've failed.
You've progressed, and you've regressed.
You've transcended, and you've descended.

Thoughts of hopelessness & worthlessness have probably entered your mind.

"I've tried", you say.
"I am nothing", you moan.

We have all been there...but stop right there.

In our individual and collective journey through life, we must never sabotage ourselves with words of defeat, even if we feel defeated.

We must never assault ourselves with shame, even if we feel ashamed.

Everytime we get knocked down, we MUST get back up again.

When I am knocked down, I do everything I can to not only get up, but to get up and push harder.

I've learned to be grateful for the backward steps. They sharpen me and keep me focused.

Like a bow & arrow, they launch me forward with double the power, double the determination and double the conviction.

I used to think that I could do all of that on my own. But I now realize that my strength comes from The One who created me.

So, the question is not "who do you think you are?" It is "WHOSE do you know you are?"

You are a MAGNIFICENT, RESILIENT and BLESSED child of the Almighty God.

THAT is who you are.

KEY TAKEAWAY:

Magnificent,

RESILIENT & BLESSED.

How can the main theme of today's message apply to my life?

What is one thing I will start, stop or continue doing as a result of today's message?

Who can I share today's message with so they might benefit also?

Additional Notes:

BREATHE, PRAY, & Focus.

Have you ever woken up, and not felt like yourself? You couldn't really describe what you were feeling, but something just felt...off. That happened to me recently. It felt like a combination of physical, emotional, mental and spiritual discomfort settling in the center of my body.

I didn't like it, and I knew that something had to be DONE about it. There was no way that I would become content or normalize such feelings.

So what did I do? (I'm so glad you asked)

First, I BREATHED. Deeply. Deliberately. Purposefully. Oxygen is life, and I needed to flood my body with it. When we are stressed, we tend to breath in a very shallow manner. (Job 33:4)

Second, I PRAYED. I went to my knees, bowed low and praised the Most High...out loud. It's amazing how outward worship can calm inward distress. If complaints can be done out loud, then my praises should be also. (Psalms 34:1)

Third, I FOCUSED. On what? Everything and everyone I am blessed to have in my life. Including YOU who are reading this right now. I did an inventory: Health. Home. Family. Even down to the ability to chew and swallow my own food! (Philippians 4:8)

Whenever that feeling of unexplainable discomfort comes lurking around, remember to BREATHE, PRAY & FOCUS.

KEY TAKEAWAY:

I am Blessed!

AND SO ARE YOU!

How can the main theme of today's message apply to my life?

What is one thing I will start, stop or continue doing as a result of today's message?

Who can I share today's message with so they might benefit also?

Additional Notes:

BE
grateful.

I've lived long enough to know that hard work and determination lead to success. I've grinded, hustled, sweat and cried through MANY hills and valleys, both personally and professionally.

I can stand now and be very grateful for the immense blessings that I have. From my bride...to my children...to my business...to my health...even to the influence that I'm allowed to have with people I've never even met.

But NONE of those blessings would have been possible without a blesser. Or better yet: The Blesser.

I fully acknowledge that if I have it, then it was God who gave it to me. Period.

Another dimension of gratitude opened when I realized that my daily purpose is to manifest what The Most High put inside of me. Therefore, whatever I have is not really mine. I am merely a steward who is entrusted to share what was first shared with me.

And so it is with you.

That's the cycle: Be grateful when receiving and be even more grateful when giving. None of it is ours anyway.

KEY TAKEAWAY:

Gratefully

receive.

GRACIOUSLY GIVE.

How can the main theme of today's message apply to my life?

What is one thing I will start, stop or continue doing as a result of today's message?

Who can I share today's message with so they might benefit also?

Additional Notes:

DON'T STOP UNTIL
you get it.

No one can MAKE you believe that something is important. They can tell you, scold you and even punish you. But you still have to arrive at that sacred place and declare, "This is important; therefore, I will treat it as such." And when that happens, NOTHING can stop you.

In September of 2006, I took a major leap of faith. I decided to leave a company that I grew up in and start my own business. Now, let's be clear. I didn't have savings to speak of. There was no severance to fall back on.

Nothing.

I was literally leaving a secure, monthly job to start over. I gave myself one month to earn the same salary that I was making in the job I just left. One month!

So, I gave myself two options: Succeed or Succeed. That was it. And I meant it.

For the next several weeks, I worked non-stop and barely slept more than three hours during that period. I made a list of potential clients, built a website, set-up contracts, wrote training courses and developed s consulting framework...all by myself.

The adrenaline was HIGH!

Bottom line: I made over half my annual salary between Oct and December of 2006. And then over 3 times my previous annual salary the following year.

I'm not writing this to impress you, but rather to impress upon you what YOU are capable of!

It's amazing what can be done when you've given yourself no other option but to succeed.

That experience taught me that success has far more to do with DESIRE than capability. Do you want it bad enough?

KEY TAKEAWAY:

Decide what is important to you,

AND DON'T STOP UNTIL

YOU GET IT.

How can the main theme of today's message apply to my life?

What is one thing I will start, stop or continue doing as a result of today's message?

Who can I share today's message with so they might benefit also?

Additional Notes:

COURAGE DARES YOU TO
try.

The late Maya Angelou once said that, "Courage is the most important of all the virtues, because without courage you can't practice any other virtue consistently."

Whether the virtue is love, honesty, kindness, ambition or any other...courage dares you to TRY.

Without courage, you get frozen and wonder, "what if I fail"? With courage, you know that NOT trying is failure itself.

Without courage, you will do what you've ALWAYS done. With courage, you will think of ways to innovate and reinvent yourself.

It demands action regardless of the circumstances.

Courage makes you GET UP when you feel like staying down.

Courage makes you SPEAK UP when you feel like staying quiet.

Courage makes you MOVE FORWARD when you feel like staying still.

Disappointments and setbacks can lull you into thinking "why bother?" But courage makes you stand strong and declare "why not?"

To all of the courageous people reading this, YOU inspire me. Your courage will always take you farther than you ever imagined.

KEY TAKEAWAY:

Onward!

How can the main theme of today's message apply to my life?

What is one thing I will start, stop or continue doing as a result of today's message?

Who can I share today's message with so they might benefit also?

Additional Notes:

NEVER BE ASHAMED OF
your source.

A note to my Encourager:

My Savior. My Redeemer. My Rock. My King. Jesus Christ.

Thank you, Lord, for blessing me in unimaginable ways. I am because You are. You took a hot mess like me and cleaned me up. NOBODY can do that like You.

Every post. Every article. Every keynote. Every video. EVERYTHING I do is inspired by You.

You did not give me a mission to reach millions of people. Instead, you have commanded me to reach one person...today. That's it.

One person who will feel what You have shared with me. In truth, every "like", "love" and comment is actually for You.

Lord, my only request is that you grant me the daily mindfulness to allow myself to be decreased so that You can be increased.

May I never get tired of openly acknowledging my relationship with You.

KEY TAKEAWAY:

I am

BECAUSE

You are.

How can the main theme of today's message apply to my life?

What is one thing I will start, stop or continue doing as a result of today's message?

Who can I share today's message with so they might benefit also?

Additional Notes:

LET HOPE

pull you.

The longer I live, the more I realize the importance of hope. It's tied to everything. If someone wants to discourage you, all they have to do is remove your "hope".

Without hope, you don't EXPECT anything to be better.

Without hope, you won't believe that "someone like you" can have a meaningful life.

Without hope, you'll give up looking for a fulfilling job...or starting that business that you've been dreaming of.

Cling to your hope!

Rebuke every rancid lie of hopelessness that crawls into your ear. Don't allow anyone to sprinkle seeds of discouragement around you.

Because of hope, you must BELIEVE that your next step will be better than your last step. Therefore, take another step. Always take another step. Refuse to be hopeless.

We all have moments of discouragement. We all have seasons of scarcity. But hope will ALWAYS pull us forward.

On the days when you feel weary...have hope.

On the days when you don't feel like moving...have hope.

Let hope pull you. Let faith push you. And let love move you.

KEY TAKEAWAY:

Faith.

HOPE.

Love.

How can the main theme of today's message apply to my life?

What is one thing I will start, stop or continue doing as a result of today's message?

Who can I share today's message with so they might benefit also?

Additional Notes:

WHO WILL YOU EXTEND
grace to today?

Grace. Undeserved goodwill towards others.

As I look at my life, and ponder where I am, it is so clear that grace has been the driving factor.

Back in 2008, I was in the midst of my doctoral program. I was in school full-time, running a very busy speaking business, AND traveling non-stop. I was beyond overwhelmed. As a result, I fell behind on my schoolwork and even farther behind on a classroom team project.

One day, I felt like I couldn't take the stress any longer so I called one of my classmates. I apologized for not pulling my weight and told him that I planned to take some months off from school to catch my breath.

He paused on the phone for a few seconds then said, "Nonsense. There is no way you are dropping out of this class. We've got you! We will pull together, and we'll all get through this together."

Listen...I felt the hand of God's grace on me! With tears rolling down my face, I thanked him. Then I felt a surge of rejuvenation and jumped right back into my schoolwork with renewed vigor. Grace did that!

Even as you're are reading this, your grace is driving me, sustaining me, and inspiring me.

So, the key question in all of this is...

Who will YOU extend grace to today?

KEY TAKEAWAY:
EXTEND UNDESERVED
GOODWILL
to others.

How can the main theme of today's message apply to my life?

What is one thing I will start, stop or continue doing as a result of today's message?

Who can I share today's message with so they might benefit also?

Additional Notes:

GIVE &
Receive.

One of my favorite songs is from the late, great Luther Vandross. It's called "So Amazing." The chorus is..."It's so amazing to be loved. I'd follow you to the moon in the sky above."

If my life could have a soundtrack, that song would be on it.

I must admit...I'm a MUCH better giver than receiver. It's natural for me to lavish praise, anticipate needs and give encouragement. But it's taken me years to finally get (somewhat) comfortable with receiving the same treatment.

I've learned that in my haste to lift others, I unintentionally stifled others from lifting me.

In many ways, receiving love is just as important as giving love.

So, here's my advice for the perennial "givers" out there:

When anyone wants to do something nice for you, let them.

When anyone encourages you, thank them.

When anyone wants to help you, allow them.

Give and Receive: Love is expressed in both ways.

KEY TAKEAWAY:

Selflessly Give

& GRACIOUSLY RECEIVE.

How can the main theme of today's message apply to my life?

What is one thing I will start, stop or continue doing as a result of today's message?

Who can I share today's message with so they might benefit also?

Additional Notes:

SECOND
chances.

Years ago, when I was a hotel banquet server, I always asked for opportunities to do more & learn more. I was like a sponge. Eager to soak up anything I could learn about service, food, wine and set-up.

One day, the bqt director came to me and said that my work ethic impressed him. He wanted me to be his "right hand" for an upcoming event. My job would be to organize the set-up.

The big day came, and I was scheduled to report to work at 9AM. Somehow, my alarm didn't go off and I overslept...by a lot. I didn't get to work until after 10AM. When he saw me, he had a look of sheer hurt and disappointment on his face.

He quickly interrupted my barrage of excuses and quietly said, "I was counting on you." Then he walked away.

I should have been written up, suspended or even fired. In fact, I expected it. But nothing happened. He ended up giving me another opportunity, and I seized it with both hands.

The point is that I did nothing to deserve another opportunity, but I got it anyway. If not for his willingness to forgive, coach, and give me another chance, I would not be where I am today. In many cases, undeserved grace has been the only valid explanation for my success.

KEY TAKEAWAY:

Never forget the

SECOND CHANCES THAT YOU RECEIVED ALONG THE WAY.

How can the main theme of today's message apply to my life?

What is one thing I will start, stop or continue doing as a result of today's message?

Who can I share today's message with so they might benefit also?

Additional Notes:

UNTIL I
succeed.

I graduated with my doctorate in 2010, and the journey to get there was NOT easy (nor should it have been). Specifically, the dissertation process brought me to the edges of my sanity multiple times.

As you may know, the dissertation is an exhaustive research project that is usually comprised of five chapters. The 1st three chapters are referred to as "The Proposal", and it must be approved by the University's Academic Review Board. For me, it took FIVE (count 'em)...FIVE tries before it got approved. It was rejected by the University FIVE times.

Each time it was rejected, I felt like King Kong punched me in the gut.

I put my whole heart and mind into every revision...only to be denied...again. I honestly wanted to give up on that goal and move on with my life. I was almost convinced that it would never be approved. Perhaps I wasn't meant to accomplish this goal after all.

Then I remembered an important lesson that was taught to me years prior.

If I keep going...If I don't quit...If I keep moving...I WILL SUCCEED. And that is true whether you're learning a musical instrument or saving to buy a home.

The principle is the same: Persist UNTIL you succeed.

KEY TAKEAWAY:

Two Options

SUCCEED OR SUCCEED.

How can the main theme of today's message apply to my life?

What is one thing I will start, stop or continue doing as a result of today's message?

Who can I share today's message with so they might benefit also?

Additional Notes:

EMPTY.

Zero. Nothing. Empty. That is what I am praying for this week. I don't want an abundance. Not looking for an overflow. This week, my cup does not need to run over. All I desire is to be empty...so that I can be filled.

Full cups have no room to be filled. After all, they are already full. Full of knowledge, full of experience, full of aspirations.

As I've gotten older, it has become very clear to me that only empty vessels can be filled. I've learned to appreciate emptiness. I actually yearn for it now.

My aspiration is to begin each day as an empty vessel...so that I will have room to be filled. When I am filled, I will have something to share with others. Empty vessels have nothing to give. That is why it is so important for me to be filled first...so that I can have something to share.

And my goal is to share and share and share until I have nothing left...until I am empty at the end of the day.

Then, the cycle can repeat itself the next day. Empty. Get filled. Eagerly share until I am empty again.

For me, "empty" means humility in knowing that I will never know enough. Empty means that despite degrees, certifications, experience and accolades that I will ALWAYS be a student. There will always be room for improvement.

Getting "filled" means having a deep appreciation for learning ANYTHING from anyone. I have learned important life lessons from newborn babies and 100 year olds.

Learning what to do is important. Learning what NOT to do is also important.

I often hear people talk (brag) about how many years experience they have. It's one thing to have 10 years experience. It's another thing to have 1 year experience 10 times. There is always something to learn and there is always someone to share it with.

KEY TAKEAWAY:

Learning

NEVER

Ends.

How can the main theme of today's message apply to my life?

What is one thing I will start, stop or continue doing as a result of today's message?

Who can I share today's message with so they might benefit also?

Additional Notes:

DO YOU
care?

There are many things you can teach people...and caring is not one of them. No matter how hard you try. No matter how you might plead; some people just don't care. Some people don't even care that they don't care (think about that for a minute). This is why it is critical to hold on to those people who do care. They care about doing things right the first time.

They care about the team they are fortunate to be on.

They care about the company they are a part of.

They care about the experience their customers have.

They care if the company is making money.

They care about their role.

They care enough to ask, "how can I help this team be even stronger?".

They care about coming to work prepared to uplift (and not bring down) the team morale.

They. Just. Care. Period.

May all those who care be continuously and abundantly blessed in everything they do. May favor fall fresh on their lives and their family's lives. And may YOU be a living, breathing manifestation of everything written above.

KEY TAKEAWAY:

Always

CARE.

How can the main theme of today's message apply to my life?

What is one thing I will start, stop or continue doing as a result of today's message?

Who can I share today's message with so they might benefit also?

Additional Notes:

LIFT UP
your thoughts.

Put it down.
Turn it off.
Drive past it.

Don't do anything or go anywhere that will cause you to look at yourself in shame. It's unacceptable for anyone to make you feel worthless. And it's incomprehensible to do it to yourself.

But we are humans and are prone to self-abuse at times. So what should we do when we've developed a habit of injuring ourselves with words, thoughts or behaviors that invoke shame?

How do we lift our heads when we feel like our heads are not worthy to be lifted?

How do we move ahead when we don't even feel like getting out of bed?

Here's what has worked for me, and I know it can work for you:

"Fix your thoughts on what is true, and honorable, and right, and pure, and lovely, and admirable. Think about things that are EXCELLENT and worthy of praise." Philippians 4:8

There it is: CHOOSE to focus only on things that lift you up. Make it a new habit. Only a habit can subdue a habit. Turn away from anything (or anyone) that induces shame in your life. Leave that thing right where it is. It's a choice. Always has been. Always will be.

But what if the waves of stress, anxiety and fear are all around you? CHOOSE to nourish your mind with good thoughts, until it becomes a habit. Then never stop doing it.

KEY TAKEAWAY:

Nourish your mind WITH GOOD THOUGHTS.

How can the main theme of today's message apply to my life?

What is one thing I will start, stop or continue doing as a result of today's message?

Who can I share today's message with so they might benefit also?

Additional Notes:

DO IT WITH LOVE
or leave it alone.

It's about your heart.

With all I've written about touchpoints, anticipating needs and steps of service, NONE of them can compare with your heart. Your heart is what connects with people. Your heart is what allows you to listen empathetically. Your heart is what causes you to give a genuine smile to a complete stranger.

Yes, the heart is what pushes you to love.

Love IS service, and service IS love.

Love makes you forgive...and confront...and stand up...and comfort...and reassure...and move on...and begin...and continue.

If you do ANYTHING with love, it will be very hard to fail. I believe that in my bones!

So, as you move forward, say goodbye to what was, and reach forth for what will be. Refuse to invest your time in anything if your whole heart isn't present.

KEY TAKEAWAY:

Love is service,

SERVICE IS LOVE.

How can the main theme of today's message apply to my life?

What is one thing I will start, stop or continue doing as a result of today's message?

Who can I share today's message with so they might benefit also?

Additional Notes:

The Affirmation
COLLECTION

TODAY

Today... enthusiastically and gratefully celebrate that I woke up

Today...begin by loving myself, then let that same love guide how I treat others (regardless if they deserve it or not)

Today...do one thing for one customer, with absolute perfection... then repeat

Today...tell one colleague that I value them and why

Today...tell one customer that I value them and why

Today...tell myself that I value myself and why

Today...serve each person with excellence and not adjust my eagerness, kindness or attentiveness based on how "important" I believe a particular customer is.

Today...make it my minimum expectation to exceed everyone else's expectations

Today...don't just serve...don't just engage...but truly honor each person I serve.

Today...graciously appreciate that no one else in the world can serve exactly like me, and be proud of that difference.

And when the day comes to a close, ask myself, "Did I make a positive, meaningful, and memorable difference in anyone's life today?"

LIFT ME
Higher

Push me, challenge me, inspire me.

Accept nothing less than my absolute best.

Don't accept my excuses…my seemingly logical reasons for not doing it right the first time.

Tell me that you expect more from me.

Tell me that you believe in me, and treat me accordingly.

Give me opportunities to grow, and expect me to succeed.

Hold me accountable to your high expectations.
Accept nothing less.

You are a shaper, a molder, a curator of talent.

As a result of you, my present and my future are that much brighter.

Even when I don't see it, you remind me there is more for me to do…more for me to accomplish.

Lift me…Lift me higher.

Insist on excellence.

Refuse to waver.

I believe in you, because you believe in me.

Lift me higher.

SACRED
Ground

This is where healing takes place.

This is where caring takes place.

This is where the ultimate expression of hospitality takes place.

Everything I say and do should declare that "I see you...I honor you...and you haveunconditional worthiness".

Let there be no gossip. Let there be no negativity.

Let us only lift each other up, as we lift up those we take care of.

Let us be grateful that there are people who entrust us with their health. People who need us and depend on us.

May we never take that for granted or grow complacent.

This ground is not sacred because of my degrees, or certifications, or expertise.

It is sacred because "caring" happens here. Healing happens here. Love happens here.

From this day forward, I will consistently care for others, care for my colleagues, and care for myself.

As long as I have breath, I will do everything I can to keep this ground sacred.

SMILE, LIKE THE SUN

Is Shining

Through You

Smile, like the sun is shining through you.

Serve, like the one you are serving is a king or queen.

Inspire, like the words you say will move someone to dream bigger.

Honor, like everything you do must be done right the first time.

Lift, like your encouragement is all someone needs to climb higher.

Shine, like every deed you do will illuminate everything around you.

Encourage, like you are all that is needed to bring someone out of despair.

Share, like one thing you give today will positively transform someone else's day.

Magnify, like your passion is to show people a brighter version of themselves.

Engage, like each relationship you build is a sacred one that must be nurtured.

So, smile, serve, inspire, honor, lift, shine, encourage, share, magnify and engage.

Do themdaily; Do themfrequently; Do them withlove in your heart.

Most of all...Do themwithout expecting anythingin return.

Go, the sun is shining through you.

TODAY IS NOT
the Day.

Today is not the day.

If anyone is going to do a shortcut, it won't be me.

I refuse to do my job halfway. Not today.

There are all kinds of ways for things to go wrong. Let them be accidents.

I will not allow myself to intentionally do less than I'm capable of doing.

In the past, my mood dictated how I worked. I allowed myself to be distracted far too often by the lure of mediocrity.

After all, it's easy to be mediocre, but starting today, mediocrity and I don't see eye to eye. I have a new allergy and it's called average, and I don't need to go to a pharmacy for the medication because I already have it.

It's called conviction. It's called passion. It's called zeal. It's called honor.

My minimum expectation will be to exceed everyone else's expectations.

In fact, my expectation will be to exceed my own expectations, not tomorrow, but today.

My teammates and I work hard and I respect their efforts together. We stand strong and I will not be the weak link in the chain. Not today.

I will not be the one who makes excuses, not today. I will not be the one who grunts and complains. Not today.

I will not be the one who burdens my teammates with undone work. Not today.

I will not be the one who doesn't follow up with customers, when I said I would. Not today.

Excellence is not what I will accomplish in the future. Excellent is what I do today.

I am here today, so I will love today.

And I will be a blessing today because I am alive today.

BURN
The Bridge

Why are you looking back? The past is the past and it cannot be undone. Yes, you can learn from it. Yes, you can assess areas to improve…but your true success does not live in the past; nor does it live in the future. It lies in what you do today. Today, as in right now.

So many of us are afraid to step forward today because we are anchored to what happened yesterday. Burn the bridge.

Bridges don't have to be bad. Bridges can be beautiful. They can help you get from one place to the next. But now, you've crossed that bridge, and there's nothing to go back to. Burn the bridge.

By leaving the bridge intact, you might be tempted to go back. But there is NOTHING for you back there. Burn the bridge.

Focus on what you must do now to get to your vision. The vision is ahead of you, and your past is behind you. Back there…in that former place…over the bridge.

You probably thought that you would stay there. You probably thought it was too hard to get out. You probably thought that "people like you" didn't deserve anything better.

You were wrong. If you are reading this, you are here…not back there.

If you can feel what I am conveying, you are here…not back there.

So…Burn the bridge. Burn it! It's gone. Up in smoke. Never look back. Just focus on what you need to do now…to get to your next bridge.

SING IT
Out Loud

Sing it out loud. Sing it with your eyes closed tight. Sing it with your head raised and tears rolling down your face. Sing YOUR song with pride...and passion...and purity.

Is your "song" how you serve? Is it how you give? Is it how you encourage? Is it how you teach? Is it how you share?

Whatever your song may be, do it all the way. No one else has to understand your song. That's ok. It's not for anyone else to understand but you.

It was a gift given to you by God, and now it is your responsibility to bless others with it.

Sing your song all day. Sing it everyday. Sing it until you know ALL the words.

This world has been waiting for YOU to sing your song. And when you start, don't stop.

Never stop.

Always sing your song with that beautiful voice that ONLY YOU can provide.

MOUNTAIN
Climber

Mountains are majestic. They are beautiful...and grand...and daunting. Are mountains meant to be looked at? Admired? Feared? Or climbed?

We ALL have mountains in our lives. Every single one of us.

Whether your mountain is called self-control or depression or anything else, there is a way to climb it. That way is comprised of one word with two syllables: Today.

The path to climbing your mountain starts with taking one step... today. Not tomorrow, but today. Focus all of your energy on today. Nothing else matters.

Having a vision of that mountain being climbed is great. But the vision is not "today".

Today! Climb that. Conquer that. Celebrate that. Thank God for that. Then when (not if) you take that step today, it will be so much easier to take the next step tomorrow.

ME
First

As I live each day, my goal is not to wait for what I can get...it is to see what I can give.

I was allowed to wake up today; many others were not.
I am allowed to walk and talk today; many others can not.

I will use the gifts I've been blessed with today; many others will not.

And because such favor has fallen on me, my mission is to serve... first.

I will encourage first.

I will love first.

I will help first.

I will lift first.

I will give first.

Even more than that...

I will open doors first.

I will show gratitude first.

I will give recognition first.

ME First!

I have no right to expect ANYTHING from ANYONE whom

I haven't given something to first.

I did not work for the air that I breathe.

I had nothing to do with the sun shining on me.

I had nothing to do with the sun shining on me.

My heart is not beating because of anything I did.

They are all gifts. And beautiful gifts at that.

Gifts that I never asked for.

Gifts that I receive everyday.

I am alive, so I will live.

I have received, so I will give...first.